I0191365

Sunset Liminal
Spring 2016
Volume 3

Head Editor & Poetry Editor
Greg Scheiber

Guest Prose Editor
Candise Henson

Managing Editor
Kate Gulden

Cover Art "Growth"
by Jessica Frank

Sunset Liminal Press Logo by Chris Balzano

ISBN-10: 0692678034
ISBN-13: 978-0692678039
Published in Silver Spring, Maryland by Sunset Liminal Press

Letter from the Editor

Dearest Reader,

     A letter like this seems to require much in the way of pomp and circumstance, but, being less than a fan of formality, I will take it upon myself to reject such complexities and, instead, invite you to enjoy a palatable selection of poetry dabbled with, for the first time in Sunset Liminal history, a generous serving of prose.

     Before I discuss the intricacies of the work within, however, I wish to thank the people who put their work into our (often jumbled) hands. Without you, we could not exist, and we are therefore indebted to you.

     As I read the prose submissions for this issue, I encountered what can only be described as an editor's utopia: everything I loved connected. The narratives you will find in this issue speak to one another. They swell with a sense of urgency and yet are helplessly pinioned, desperate to escape a moment, a dream journal, a memory, a lifestyle. They are wings under domes, claustrophobic and monotonous. For this reason, they are truly human stories—pure, raw, real—ready to be bitten and savored, and so with the blessings of the authors and the assistance of my fellow staff members, I offer them to you.

Candise W. Henson

Candise W. Henson
Guest Prose Editor

Table of Contents

Prose

Carl Boon lives and works in Izmir, Turkey. His poems appear in dozens of magazines, most recently *Two Thirds North*, *Jet Fuel Review*, *Blast Furnace*, and the *Kentucky Review*.

Details

One of us is staring
at the fifth-floor window
of the Green Sea apartments.

A woman inside
has just finished a cap
for her grandson, has laid the table
for a man who can't stand her.

Absorbed in racing forms
and the news on Channel 7,
he yawns at the lentil soup.

One of us might know
the way his wrists fall
across the tablecloth, the rose-
colored one Aunt Mehtap brought

from Sivas in 1972.
The details are: the edges frayed
in the '80s, and the center holds

a burned circle
she usually covers with flowers—
lilies, crysanthememums,
or roses, depending on the season.

He wouldn't know she keeps
a stack of letters in her dresser
written in her grandson's hand.

One of us imagines
those letters and cries.
The world inside her
takes no such expression,

no beauty at all,
except when she's asleep, curling
her fingers against three blankets.

Slovakia Story

As the Slovak poet said
over his glass of *slivovica*,
the earth turns on an axis
of three: what we hold,
what we want, and why
the Damson plums ripen
in August only to slide
from girls' fingers.

I made love to a girl
in Stupava once who went
spinning to a garden
thereafter. Her white skirt
showed her white thighs,
and she muttered words
I could never understand.
The vowels were hard,

the plum trees shone
in the sun, and the women
hauled baskets too heavy
for them. In the distance
the villagers laughed,
their fingers plum-stained,
their dreams of other worlds
blocked by the hills.

J. Ryan Hibbett's work has appeared in *Atlanta Review*, *LIT*, *Eclectica*, *Codex*, *Ladowich*, *Willow Springs*, and other periodicals.

A Lesson in Seismology

Those trains. I was soaking in Epsom
when the conch shell exploded
across the linoleum. The cat's mouth
parted mutely at the furor, outlining
the barbed face of another cat.

Truly they scared me. If the tusker
in the museum could jiggle Earth
ten miles away, then Christ . . . what
could I do but suck my thumb
as those charred wheels pulverized
the junebugs, flaking sparks
like campion seeds
over the windless prairie.

Oh Snidely Whiplash! It's not like
peace comes floating back
as they diminish; some part of you
gets dragged off flapping
toward the next town, leaving
this one to blemish the trail
like a set of cowbones.

When it's over you hear the sewers
weep. You poke your head out
and stare down the tracks, sewn
crudely to the planet's scalp. "Your
bag" you want to call at the vacancy,
even as yours ears lift, like the
elephants', for the next storm.

Roy

Roy came knocking late. What
did I know? I stood scratching
my neck at the threshold, my
one heat vent chortling. The
slipshod caravan exiting his
mouth bemused me, each word
staggering the throat's stairs,
the tongue's construction
beam, then teetering merrily
at the precipice. I nodded
floors into place as they fell,
steering home my orphanage
of squinting Magoos. What did I
salvage? A cop. A husband. Some-
body's dad. Maybe that's why
when he fitted my throat to his
hand, cupped like a monkey
wrench, it felt almost tender—
some hoary testament of control.
The next day a bag of Reese's
crimsoned the doorstep, half-
gone. "Roy" I breathed cogently
at the day moon. "Town drunk."

Peripheral

How I loved having cavities filled, my
arms spiraling like Milky Way tendrils
under the chirping fluorescents. Chin-
ward: a sprawling sea-bib. Sidelong
the perched hygienist, quiet and true
as a punkah wallah. Gravely I pulled
the nitrous in. The mouth was left
to its instruments, the mind escorted
to a private study of the periphery.
Flashes of chrome. Latex hands. And
this: the queer amphibian seated
on my drinking nose. Wider? Yes
wider, eye to eye with the amber
space lamp, unfurled in all its jointed
espionage from a dimpled ceiling. Had
my lip dropped onto my chest like a
stage curtain? Soft rock wormed
the intercom as I came sullenly back,
my senses rallied to a handshake. Soon
I would enter the waiting room, strange
and light, as if I had just kicked off
bowling shoes. But oh to be the flat-
tened creature. Lost in the gleaming
tackle and the rigmarole. Slackened.
Mined. Brought at last on slow gears
to a blossoming cup. Told to rinse.

Crumbs

When I airlift a mouse from my pail
his eyes are raisins. His deathwater
puddles around him in the palm's grave.

There are worlds the vacuum
cannot reach. Bantam
things, flaked
by the butter knife, let
drop by a hammering set of teeth.

Blindly the foot, propped
on the ottoman, scrapes
free the single grain. Bravely
the wrist fishes the darkness
for the remote.

This life is crummy, the Beaver
explains. His brother consoles:

morsel comes from the French,
meaning bite. See them huddled there
Beav on the communion tray. Last

suppers for star-crossed mice.

Leah Stenson is a published poet, Board Member of Friends of William Stafford and Tavern Books, and coordinator and host of the prestigious Studio Series Poetry Reading and Open Mic in Portland. She is the author of two chapbooks, *The Turquoise Bee* and *Heavenly Body*, and the co-editor of two anthologies, *Reverberations from Fukushima: 50 Japanese Poets Speak Out* and *Alive at the Center: Contemporary Poems from the Pacific Northwest*.

Inokashira Park

Kichijoji, Tokyo

Circles on the rain-dimpled pond
expand, intersect, like kimono patterns.
Pitter-patter on a plastic umbrella
evokes memories of a nursery song
Japanese mothers sing to soothe
children house-bound on rainy days.
Pedestrians flow across a footbridge
past white swan paddle boats
huddled together at the water's edge.

I could dwell forever in this *ukiyoe*
moment, fragment of a floating world.

Joe Baumann possesses a Ph.D. in English from the University of Louisiana at Lafayette, where he served as the editor-in-chief of *Rougarou: an Online Literary Journal* and the *Southwestern Review*. He is the author of *Ivory Children: Flash Fictions,* and his work has appeared in *Tulane Review, Willow Review, Hawai'i Review,* and many others, and is forthcoming in *Jelly Bucket, Lunch Ticket,* and others. He teaches composition, literature, and creative writing at St. Charles Community College in St. Charles, Missouri.

Pinwheel

1

From their spot atop the Ferris wheel that stands in the center of the parking lot, Rhea and Agatha can hear the carnival sounds below: the Scrambler groaning and spinning, chucking bodies against metal, people screaming, shoulders smashed together, hands clutching at the safety guard. The sound of laughter and giggling swirling up into the summer air in a cyclone of noise, carried away into the blue sky. Everyone wafting through the air with the sun shining down as they spin. Agatha, looking over the plastic side of their bucket seat, stares down at the roving Scrambler. From where she sits, it
seems to move faster than usual.

"Why do people always scream on those things?" Rhea says. The wind swallows up her voice.

Agatha turns to her. "Because it's a thrill ride. You're supposed to scream." Below them, large electric generators buzz like a hive of mutant, gargantuan bees.

"I don't scream. Do you?"

"I don't ride those rides."

"You used to."

"I guess I don't want to scream anymore." Agatha turns away, bites her lip. "We've been up here a long time. I think something's wrong." Looking down again, she cranes her neck: a line of people wait to board the Ferris wheel. Some are eating cotton candy; a few shade their eyes from the sun. She can't see the attendant in his bright yellow t-shirt.

"It's not like it's a surprise." Rhea flicks a strand of hair from her mouth. "People know what they're getting into. They climb in, spin around, then get spit back out."

A moment of silence falls over them as the breeze stops. More noise crowds up toward them: the crank and creak of the flying swings next to the

14

Ferris wheel, stirring and tossing people round and round. Agatha watches them, mostly children and teenagers, arms outstretched like wings, legs flopping beneath the plastic seats that remind her of oversized, colorful diapers. She wonders where those kids hope to fly off to. She tries to focus in on a single, random swing as it cantilevers around, but doing so is dizzying.

"I guess it's like an emotional release," Agatha says, blinking.

"It's just a ride," Rhea says.

Agatha shrugs. "What does it matter if they scream or not, anyway?"

They both look out at the soccer field next to the parking lot and watch clumps of people milling about, dashing across the grass. Voices commingle and are then drowned out by the generators and distance.

Tents, carnival-style with red and white stripes, dot the perimeter of the field. Rhea points toward one of them, near the school building at the northern end of the parking lot.

"Dad's over there, I think. Third tent from the right."

"I know, Rhea."

"You think he's disappointed?"

"About what?"

"You know, that I didn't work it with him this year."

Agatha turns to her. "You haven't worked the beer booth with him in years. Why would he care now?"

Rhea reaches into her pocket, pulling out a crumpled pack of cigarettes and twists, rocking the seat, producing a lighter from the other.

"Could you be careful?" Agatha says, reaching her hand out for the guard rail.

"What? Scared?"

"No," Agatha says. She watches Rhea work the lighter, shielding it under one hand to guard from the breeze.

"I thought you were quitting."

"And I thought you had to go to work today, but here you are."

Agatha looks toward the entrance of the school. A bulky queue snakes in through the double doors, her mother somewhere among them. Agatha tries to find her in the crowd, squints through the sunlight, but can't pick out her mother's salt-and-pepper hair, her thin shoulders, her skin light and pale and freckled like Agatha's. It never tans into the supple gold of Rhea's complexion, instead always burning and turning a red that matches her hair.

Rhea looks toward the field, trying to find her father, wondering if she can make him out under the shaded cover of one of the tents, but she knows the angle isn't right.

"How is work, anyway?" Rhea says, cigarette dangling from one side of her mouth.

Agatha wants to tell her it's great, that it's going really well, but she knows Rhea knows that waiting tables is the same every day. It's fine. Never good, never bad. Just a dull, gray fine. But before she can speak, the Ferris wheel lurches, and, with a squeal of metal, the sisters plunge forward, the ride carrying them down.

2

Agatha knows she shouldn't have let Rhea convince her to ride the Ferris wheel.

"It's just a Ferris wheel. It'll be ten minutes. What else do you have to do?" she remembers Rhea saying, an eyebrow raised behind her sunglasses. Agatha suspects Rhea wears them to hide the look that reeks of pity, of sympathy for the younger sister who still lives at home. A look that means Rhea is thinking of her own happy escape, her moving on to her own independent life. Rhea had her hand on her hip, asking Agatha what it was about the Ferris wheel she was so afraid of.

So Agatha said fine, yes. Let's go, she said.

Now here she is. When the Ferris wheel spins down after the pendulous stop at the top, they swoop toward the ground but then the ride keeps going, their seat crawling back up, and they come to a lurching stop back where they started.

"Well, great," Rhea says. She leans back and inhales on her cigarette. Agatha glances at her and sighs. She doesn't care that her sister smokes, except that she always says she's quitting, that every pack is her last one, she promises, she swears. She's been saying the same thing for two years.

When Agatha looks over the side of the seat, things look amiss below: the Scrambler is swinging around on its axis fast—too fast. The seat clusters spiral around with heavy momentum, and the thunkathunkathunk of the craning metal sounds like a monitor tracking a fast-rising heartbeat. She shakes her head and closes her eyes for a moment, placing her fingers on the bridge of her nose.

"What's going on?" she thinks aloud.

Rhea shakes her head. "How should I know?"

A prickling feeling crawls up Agatha's neck at the coolness in her sister's voice. She looks toward Rhea, and she can see a distant, empty look on her face. Agatha scans the front of the school building for her mother, where Agatha knows she is waiting to pay for tickets for dinner. She stands

16

on the hot concrete alone, and every time Agatha tells her mother she'll stand with her, wait in line at her side, she waves Agatha off.

Agatha turns back to Rhea. "What time are we supposed to meet Mom and Dad? It's gotta be soon, doesn't it?"

"No idea."

"What time is it, anyway?"

"Left my purse in my car."

Agatha squints at her, wondering how she can be so calm.

"Do you even care if we're late?"

"Of course I do." Rhea turns to Agatha and peels off her sunglasses. "But do you think Mom won't understand? Do you think she'll think we just skipped out? Or, what, that Dad won't find her? Do you not think they can handle eating by themselves, together?"

Agatha sighs and crosses her arms.

"Of course I do."

"Then why are you so worried? I want to eat with them, too, but what exactly are we supposed to do?"

Agatha pictures her mother standing in line. Every night when Agatha gets home from work—even the late shift, when her mother should already be asleep—there she is, waiting for her in the kitchen. They sit and drink wine and her mother asks Agatha how her shift was. She's been asking the same question for five years, ever since Agatha first took the job, when she was eighteen, returning to the restaurant and its greasy dishes and disgruntled cooks over winter and summer breaks during college. Agatha always tells her stories, then asks her mother what she did all evening, and her mother, a vacant look on her face, tells Agatha about the loads of laundry washed, the news watched, the rerun
of that police procedural she left on even though she'd seen it before and remembered who did it. They sit up late, after her father has shuffled off to bed, talking about the same things, over and over in a loop.

"I think we're supposed to meet them at five," she says.

"Are you sure? I think Dad said six."

"How would he know better than Mom?"

"Why couldn't he?"

"She's the one that organizes it while he's busy working that stupid booth."

"So volunteering is stupid, huh?"

"You know that's not what I mean."

"Well, it's what you said."

"I just don't want to miss dinner."

"Mom won't mind if we're late."

"Yes she will." She sits up straight. "She tells me all the time. She told me last night after I got off work that she was looking forward to it."

"Yeah, well, she told me, too, when we had lunch last week."

"You had lunch last week?"

Rhea looks over the edge of her sunglasses. "Yes, Agatha, we did. As hard as it may be for you to believe, I do talk to our mother."

"I just—"

"What? She didn't mention it during your nightly talk?"

Agatha looks down. The line of people waiting to get on the Ferris wheel has grown thicker, bulging into an unruly blob. She can't see the line's start, and she wonders if the man in the yellow shirt has returned, if anyone is working to free them from the ride. Agatha thinks of the times she wakes up at night to get a glass of water and finds her mother asleep on the couch. To escape your father's snoring, her mother says. It sounds like a rusted bellows. Sometimes Agatha can hear her father's noises through the cracked bedroom door, a sliver of shadow peeking through.

"I wonder if they're happy," she says.

Rhea looks toward her. "Why wouldn't they be?"

"I don't know. They just don't seem like it."

"What does that mean?"

"I don't know. Mom seems stuck, I guess."

Rhea crosses her arms. "She seems happy to me. They're still together, aren't they?"

Agatha thinks for a moment, trying to retrace her conversations with her mother, digging through the spinning memories that flash around in her head. Does she remember a comment somewhere from her mother, a brief blip of emptiness in her eyes?

She can picture a look on her mother's face, the drooping sag under her lower eyelids, the vacant stare toward the wall past Agatha's shoulder. But she can't put words there, can't inject her mother with some voice that will tell her what her mother feels. She's simply suspended there, a silent portrait.

Why wouldn't she tell Agatha about having lunch with Rhea?

"Well," Agatha says.

But before she can say more, the Ferris wheel begins to turn.

3

Agatha shades her eyes against the sun, which is starting to fall

18

toward the roofs beyond the field.

"We've been up here forever," she says. The undersides of her thighs are slippery and she feels the stupor of constant sitting, her muscles achy and stiff. Her legs are used to constant movement, standing and threading between tables and chairs, balancing plates and trays on her arms. She looks at Rhea: calm, legs still. Agatha's are bouncing, shaking with cramps.

"What about when the sun goes down?" Agatha bites her lip.

"You really think we'll be up here that long?"

"Why wouldn't we be?"

A crowd has formed around the Ferris wheel, people pointing. The Scrambler and swings keep rocketing around, speed growing, riders shaken about as they crunch against one another.

Rhea looks toward the soccer field. "Hey. I think I see Dad." She points out toward one of the openings in the chain-link fence. The man she thinks is their father stands with a small cluster of people, a good six inches taller than the rest of them.

"He's not the same, you know."

"What does that mean?"

Their seat sways back and forth, creaking, a low moan with each swing.

Agatha points toward the school. "Mom told me once. He used to be different."

"Working a nine to five isn't easy, you know. Trust me."

"I don't think she's happy."

"She's not lonely."

"All he does is work, though."

"How do you know she's unhappy? He works hard."

"She tells me stuff. You just couldn't understand."

"They seem fine to—what does that mean?"

The sun keeps creeping away, slinking out of reach. Rhea and Agatha stare forward, pushing against the sides of their tiny carriage. Maybe it will burst open and they can each go tumbling down on either side, the Ferris wheel between them. Just get away.

But the plastic holding them in does not give.

A fresh breeze kicks up behind Rhea and Agatha, lifting their hair up at the same time as the Ferris wheel moves again.

4

Rhea begins to wonder if she will ever get off the Ferris wheel. She doesn't remember so much time passing, unlike her work days, where the hours on the clock drip by as she sits at her desk, staring at a computer screen.

She's out of cigarettes, which, she thinks, is probably for the best. Rhea wants to quit, but she's glad Agatha is no longer staring at her with the snide self-satisfaction she has in knowing her sister is an addict.

"How did you convince me to ride this thing?" Rhea whispers to herself, glancing at Agatha, wishing she could just get down. "I hate these rides."

"Are Mom and Dad down there?" Agatha's voice is crinkled, weak as though it will squeak and rust and stop working soon. Rhea wonders why she asks; the parking lot is dim now, and the crowd that has grown beneath the Ferris wheel is an opaque sea of upturned faces. Rhea wonders why Agatha thinks she can see anything that Agatha can't see herself.

The lights lining the rides have snapped on, tiny neon explosions that whirl around in looping, psychedelic streams, whirling splashes of tie dye colors. The tents on the soccer field are illuminated by bulbs strung up along the red and white tops, the color of yellowed smoker's teeth.

Rhea wonders why no one has come for them. No fire trucks, no police. No one acknowledging their plight except for the bevy of faces packed together below them like a jostling concert crowd, and she is washed in anger at the inactivity. The parking lot, the soccer field, the school: they're all lit up by the nauseating lights of the spinning rides as they careen around in the dark, flashing their pinks and greens and yellows across the brick exterior of the building. Everything turning in circles, going nowhere. Even the Ferris wheel, lit up and immobile like a beacon attracting attention but no action.

She thinks about what Agatha said: emotional release. She doesn't buy it.

She crumples the empty pack in her hand and considers tossing it into the night, but instead she rubs her thumb over the glossy cellophane.

"Need a cigarette?"

"No."

"What happened to quitting? Like, last year?"

"What's it matter to you?"

"Mom quit on her own, you know. No start and stop and start again."

"Yeah, twenty years after she promised Dad she would."

"What are you talking about?"

"She never told you?" Rhea smiles and tells Agatha about their

20

mother's promises, telling their father she'd quit as soon as they got married, how she stopped smoking finally when she got pregnant with Rhea, but then started again, only stopping for good when she was pregnant again with Agatha. How their parents fought about it all the time.

"Oh."

"So she never told you."

"No. She didn't."

"She told me a few years ago."

"Probably when she wanted you to quit, huh?"

Rhea is glad not to live at home anymore. She needed her freedom, but she thinks Agatha is happy there, always talking to their mother late into the night, whispering secrets to one another. She's tried more than once to tell Agatha how much better she must have it with her flexible schedule and low stress job as a waitress, how much better off she is than Rhea, who is mired in a nine to five desk job with little upward mobility.

Of course she doesn't tell Agatha how much she hates what she does, that she relishes the lunches she gets to have with her mother, getting out of her cramped office to be with someone besides the coworkers she sees eight hours every day.

Rhea shrugs. "Well, now you know."

Neither of them speaks, and Rhea listens to the whir of the carnival rides, their engines screaming at a high, buzzing pitch. Like little banshees, monsters from some other world.

"I feel so bad," Agatha says.

"What? For what?"

"For Mom. She just wants us to go to dinner, talk, eat, be a family. But it's over by now. They close dinner at seven."

"Why is it so important to you?"

"It's important to her."

"She'll get over it. Why can't you?"

"No, she won't."

She's always worrying about Mom and Dad, Rhea thinks. She tries to tell Agatha that Mom is fine, but she always shakes her head, dismissive, as if she knows their parents and Rhea doesn't.

"Whatever."

The neon bulbs from the rides below don't quite reach the top of the Ferris wheel, but their glow bubbles up under their feet. Agatha and Rhea are being plunged into the heavy darkness of night as the sun's last rays fade away. No one has tried to reach out to them, to tell them what's happening. The Ferris wheel simply idles, a growling, immobile wheel that can only spin in place like a tire trapped in mud.

Rhea hears Agatha sniffle and is about to ask her what could possibly be wrong when the ride lurches forward. But then the Ferris wheel stops, just below the peak of the ride, exactly where the seat in front of them had been moments ago. Rhea wants to scream out in exultation, but she bites her lip, waiting to see what Agatha does first.

5

Every few minutes the Ferris wheel croaks, a belching toad pushing them forward. The flashy lights of the ride begin creeping up Rhea and Agatha's legs toward their faces. Agatha watches as two boys escape the Ferris wheel, emerging from beneath the ride. They are swallowed up by the onlookers. Now everyone on the picnic grounds stares up at the Ferris wheel, faces engulfed in the ride's bright lights. No one waits for other rides. The only noise is that of the Ferris wheel and the murmuring from the people collected on the ground. The silence from the Scrambler and swings and the generators is deafening.

"Dad's down there," Rhea says, leaning over the carriage.

"I can see Mom." Agatha slumps. "I don't think she can see us."

Their parents' faces are shiny under the blanket of carnival lights. They pulsate with the pink and green energy of the bulbs.

The Ferris wheel groans again, and when it stops, their seat is swaying on the underside of the ride, the lights neon halos above their faces now. Their bodies are caught up in the glow, on display, their faces covered in the cascade of hues blistering off the rides. Agatha bites her cheek. Rhea purses her lips. The noise of the gathered crowd grows, and the whole blacktop looks as though it is covered in people, all the nooks and crannies around the rides, the rigged carnival games, the bright food trucks that emanate the smell of fryer dough: everything covered, filled in by seething, whispering voices that watch the ride.

"Where did all these people come from?" Rhea asks.

Their carriage moves again; in one rotation, the ride will end. The lights are brighter, blinding like heat lamps, and with none of the rides moving, the sisters can see the faces of people staring up at them, all eyes seemingly on their carriage. Skin is bright and colorful, distorted almost, misshapen. Both girls squint, as if the sun has come back. They both catch sight of their parents again, their heads above the rest of the crowd, as if they've stretched and grown, wafted above everyone else to reach out to the girls when they are released.

22

"Finally," they say at the same time.

The Scrambler starts up with a sudden cracking lurch, rocketing in a vicious circle, the engine screaming as if it's about to pop. Rhea and Agatha can feel the displaced air propelled at them, and the crowd becomes a blurry pastiche of light and dark again, shadows spinning across the eyes and faces of the spectators as the Scrambler's lights flicker around in the night.

"I can't believe I let you talk me into riding this thing."

"What? This was your idea."

They stare at one another as the Ferris wheel groans again, but they don't hear the noise.

"No, it was you."

They each try to remember the moments before they got on, as the Ferris wheel swoops them to the bottom position, but Rhea and Agatha can only think of their time atop the ride. They stare at one another, thinking of what they've done and what they should do next. Neither notices that the bar holding them in swings open as their gazes remain fixed on one another.

As they finally turn away from each other, Agatha takes a deep breath and is about to exhale when she stops. Rhea, starting to stretch her arms, freezes. They stare: the Ferris wheel is silent, its lights dark. The parking lot, desolate, is empty except for ticket stubs that tumble across the asphalt with the summer night's breeze. The Scrambler sits idle. No engine noises caress the air. They feel like children dangling there, so tiny on that vast, dark plain of blacktop, melting through time like the rocky asphalt. Agatha and Rhea look at one another, neither saying a word, their legs suspended in the air.

George Freek's poetry has recently appeared in *Limestone Journal*, *Off Course Literary Review*, *Trade West Review*, *Calamaro*, *Sisyphus Quarterly*, *The Lake*, and *The Missing Slate*. He also write plays which are published by Playscripts, Inc., Lazy Bee Scripts, and Off The Wall Plays.

Loneliness

(After Su Tung Po)

In this twilight an icy rain
looks like silver needles.
Later snow piles up
like heaps of white grain.
My bed is cold.
Wind blows the last
of November's leaves.
The birds have gone
where sun shines on the lakes.
I reach for the light,
but I can no longer write.
Who reads poetry anyway?
Young men with unreal dreams,
and old fools like me,
with nothing left to say.

On My 70th Birthday
(After Mei Yao Chen)

In darkness as thick as mud,
I can't see a thing.
The night is a black pit.
If there's a moon,
it is no more than a slit.
There's no one to
share my wine with.
I've outlived my friends.
I once wrote ignorant poems
about being alone.
I stare at a heron's nest,
which is now empty.
I might write a poem,
but what I know of herons,
wouldn't fill a cup of tea.
I've lived too long.
Herons and trees,
now mean nothing to me.

Brendan Raleigh is a senior English major at Gettysburg College. He is the Editor-in-Chief of the college's student newspaper and has worked as a contributing writer for *Celebrate Gettysburg* magazine and *Frederick Gorilla* magazine. His poetry was also featured in the Fall 2015 issue of *Sunset Liminal* (vol. 2).

Through Turner's Gap

I coasted past a curve
of clustered, spiny,
winter-barren trees,
and cut through the hazy
night at Turner's Gap.

The tall silhouette of Dahlgren Chapel
broke through the far-off outline
of the Blue Ridge Mountain Range,
its pointed tower ripping through the horizon
like a knife through plastic wrap
as I neared.

It was, as it always is,
lifeless and dark.
An owl is perched in the bell-less bell tower —
its glowing yellow eyes
the only source of light.

I eased up on the pedal
and slowed to take a look
at the old, stone church
and its searchlight-eyed sentinel.

As I did, a black and white spotted dog
padded out from across the street
and began to run alongside the car.
Its tags bobbed back and forth,
reflecting the moonlight and the darkness
alternatingly like a spinner.

The dog matched my speed,
occasionally looking over to me,
before turning
and darting into the thickets beside us.

Gibbous

At the beginning and end of every month, your eyes need to linger a little longer on the moon to tell if it is truly full. When it is not but almost is or just was and isn't anymore, it is called a gibbous moon.

As a kid, I thought the lighted part of a gibbous moon – thanks to the sum of all street lights, office buildings, and headlights or the reflection of the sun's rays – was some kind of reverse shadow of the earth. As if it was painted on, the border between light and dark drew a squished, distorted imitation of the earth. Though you couldn't see them, all along that outline, the shadow-light silhouettes of a few thousand people would show up on the moon and, a couple of seconds late, reenact the lives of earth's inhabitants. They were there, I was certain, though their everyday was far too far for any of us to see. Too far and, seemingly, too small.

And it always had to be a gibbous moon. There had to be that second where I'd wonder, "Is it full?" There had to be the earth-and-moon roundness to it and, once the incompleteness was realized, the untrue knowledge that I had been given an incomprehensible glimpse into millions of lives.

And there had to be the uncertainty that would breed curiosity.

I learned how wrong I was on all that. But once or twice a year, whenever the earth floats perfectly between the moon and the sun, I would be able to see all those lives at once. An eclipse would allow that.

If only the light were a little stronger.

Tomorrow in the Morning

Calvin had always planned to start writing in the dream journal, but, every time he had a dream worth remembering, he told himself that it was too interesting to forget.

He would think as he woke, "I won't need to write this one down. It's far too vivid. I could never forget this one." And each time, he would forget. He could never recall any of these "unforgettable" dreams, and the dream journal remained empty, aside from the inscription. It sat on his nightstand as an ornament and nothing more.

Calvin was reclining in the living room with four empty cups of coffee at his feet when, behind him, a flurry of heavy bootsteps flew down the stairs.

"What the hell is this?" Jaina asked, holding up Calvin's dream journal.

"That is the journal you bought me."

"Not a single entry, Calvin." She threw the book on his lap. "Not a single fucking entry."

"Isn't the point of a journal that it's private?"

"As a secondary function, maybe. The primary function is to fucking write in it." She threw the book into his lap.

"Look, I know how you're taking this. It isn't anything against you. It was really nice of you to get it for me. And the sessions, too. All great. I really appreciate it. You're a great sis."

"Stop bullshitting, Cal. Have you even been going to those sessions?"

"Of course."

"Well what the hell have you been telling Dr. Kaminsky? When I went, ninety percent of what we talked about were my dreams. And look at me!"

"Healthy as a clam."

"Absolutely! What have you been talking to him about?"

"Dreams."

"You haven't written a single one down."

"I mostly just make them up. Sometimes he talks about his dreams, too. Did he tell you about the one with the pencil forest?"

"You piece of shit. I'm living paycheck-to-paycheck here while you sit on your ass all day drinking coffee. Wasting a gift that I thought would help you."

Calvin shrugged. "I just think it's bullshit, Jay."

"Dad told me to take care of you. What did he tell you, huh? Did he ask you to try taking care of me?"

"Of course he did," Calvin lied.

"Then you're doing a shit job of it. I'm going to bed."

Calvin took a sip of cold coffee. Jaina was halfway up the stairs when he shouted up to her, "I already know what they mean." His sister draped her arms over the railing. Calvin continued, "I think I have to forget them."

"If you talk to a fucking doctor, you won't have anything you 'have to forget.'" She continued her way up the stairs.

He opened up the journal and read the inscription Jaina had written, then began to flip through the empty pages; his parents did not seem like they were dead and he could not decide if he preferred it like that. He placed his mug on the table and got up to go to bed.

Matt Babcock Professor. Writer. Failed breakdancer. Debut fiction collection, *Future Perfect*, forthcoming from *Queen's Ferry Press* (October 2016). Debut poetry collection, *Points of Reference*, forthcoming from Folded Word (March 2016).

Home Movies

In a water-stained shoebox
in a padlocked storage unit in Twin Falls,
my father, still a young man,
bounds like a model of modern dance
around our grainy backyard
on Sunnyside Avenue in Salt Lake City,
slashing at frantic mobs of cabbage moths
with a hand-made net, as if
slicing his scimitar of a thousand Junes
through the first of many summers
to vanish too soon under the acetate sky.
My mother tries to steady 1973,
wonders where she left the manual
to our masque. In the dark room
of small histories, the scene gets labeled
"Day Without Script," part Buster Keaton,
part comic safari, armed, as we are,
with lame apparatus of broom handles,
hooped clothes hangers, and flimsy pillowcases
that billow like the breath of butterflies.
Return, heart, to when you were
the only lens. Spirit, the crackling soundtrack.
These Super 8 dreams pin me
spread-eagle to the shade of willow trees,
millimeters from the morphology
of my dad's muttonchops, vanilla flare-legs,
and purple paisley shirt with drawstrings
criss-crossing a triangle patch
of chest fuzz. On cue, he crouches
behind a picnic table, springs up, and takes
a wild swing at heaven, then peeks in

31

at the microscopic scales on the wings
of my unborn brothers and sister.
The frame skips. The end slips free of the reel.
A shaky hand pitches us into the great
compound eye of the sun, bleaching the cyan
from our yellow afternoons, the magenta
from our laughter, souls over-exposed,
fingers shiny with the dust of a robust hatch
of what we never tire of chasing but never catch.

Cruise Poem

I'd never known the full force of ginger
till you ate a root from your won ton soup
in the Seven Seas Dining Room. Later,
I tasted that woody spice down the slope
of your back when we folded together
like oceans after torch singer Karen
Saunders in the Stardust Lounge, fair weather,

and cocktails and calypso on deck nine.
Seven days, a rigor of idleness:
Cancún hawkers, the sun a scalloped shell,
daily shuffleboard tourney at four plus
chit chat with the rich Houston clientele,
snorkeling through yellow-tailed snapper deep
into blue afternoon on Roatan

in molten sapphire bays as clear as sleep,
the heat a rare medallion on your skin.
And the souvenir smuggled home with me—
those nets of ginger scent cast in our room
as if your pores had breathed a recipe
for something more solid than the Tulum
ruins. On day five, off the starboard rail

flying fish broke the surface, skimming for
the Caribbean sun as if to sail
for miles, clipped the waves like silver dollars.
Love's evolution, I wanted to say—
I pointed, you said you didn't see, *Where?*—
isn't a matter of why some breeds fly
but when to look, how long you have to stare.

We Are A Country

of crucifixes made of white PVC pipe
stabbed in the dirt at roadside,
of chintzy pink pinwheels, brass urns
and button-eyed teddy bears
with pink tummies, prayer beads
and peace symbol pillows heaped at the foot
of pallet slats nailed into crosses
at the summit of Malad Pass,
shrines of black-eyed Susans
and supermarket mums shining
in September sun like boutounnières of blood,
of makeshift memorials on that last
dangerous curve after Castle Rock
on Highway Twenty as you approach
Mountain Home so Dave
or Emilio or Duffy can know
we think of them even though
they didn't think of themselves,
a country of vigils without vigilance,
of sideswipe and broadside and jackknife
and midnight pile-up of weekend pilgrims
who mark disaster then turn around
and overshoot the same turn,
unlike Tim Goodale, who, hearing of
Shoshoni hostiles to the south
near Massacre Rocks, steered over
a thousand wagons in safe passage
across miles of wild wasteland to the northeast,
one thinking man's quest still carved
in ruts through the sagebrush
and lava rock in a country
of rubbernecker roadkill and rumble strips,
of gin rummy and crash test dummies
for gods, for the spilled radiator fluid
of dreamy patriots, for bits of glass
twinkling in the spacious everlasting splendor
of shattered windshield skies.

Brandon Hall is a student of Gettysburg College. Nineteen now, he has been writing since fifteen with varying degrees of success. He was literature editor of his high school literary magazine, *Pulp*, for two years, and spent a year as a tutor in the writing center helping students on essays. Outside of writing he is an avid player of Dungeons and Dragons, a newbie fencer, and a frequent hiker and climber of not-very-tall things.

---

love-bitten roadmap

I think your legs
are the hundred miles I'd walk
alone
to a cold bed in a little hostel just outside of Denver

Your skin
is the cream-white silk
we'd pretend the sheets were made of until the too-soon
light of dawn ran us out of town like outlaws

Your hips
are the gentle rolling walk through which
glances and red lips and half-smiles
I'd want you

Your breasts
are lying on a Pennsylvania hilltop
whispers sinking into downy grass
at sunset

The smell of you
is a tangle of thorn-bushes a single
split raspberry leaking fragrance
that tickles at the scratches on my skin

Your hair
is night in San Antonio
shimmering in faint breeze off the river
my body thrums for me to dive

Your lips
are coming home

Allison Whittenberg is a poet and novelist (*Life is Fine*, *Sweet Thang*, and *Hollywood and Maine*, all from Random House). She lives in Philadelphia.

Why Didn't You Call Me September 11ᵗʰ?

Jean's body was drawn up in the cold. Her eyes traveled the room. Frugal, Tim kept the thermostat at 54. His nose was often red, right at the tip. It made him look like a drunk. She looked down the corners as she wondered for a moment where she was. She had one of those soprano headaches -- huge and pulsing.

Her brown body was on one side of the bed. His white one on the other. Not touching. Not on her belly. Not on her thigh.

They were quarreling, and while they did Jean looked at the four walls. They were blank. The one picture he did display was downstairs. It was of a bike trip he took when he was in college. She never asked him why that was special enough to put up, but she guessed it commemorated back when he thought of the city as an adventure instead of a cesspool.

"Jean, my brother said you should have called me."

"You weren't even in New York," she said.

"I was in an airplane."

"You were in North Carolina."

"I was over North Carolina."

Tim Flanagan was taller than her. Nearly 40, he wasn't handsome anymore. Fallen-faced. He played golf for recreation, and his body wasn't thin or thick. It was simply prematurely middle aged. Jean was average height. She kept her hair well-straightened with Dixie Peach and always looked somewhat older than she was. It was the gray hair that she did a lousy job at concealing. She had a block in the front that was solid white. Very much like Tim, with his salt and brown hair and his stiff gestures, his droopy, damp eyes, she wasn't trying to appear youthful or vigorous.

They had other things in common. Neither liked to do much. It was always dinner or a movie. Never both. Tim always paid but never bought her flowers, stuffed animals, or candy. He thought that was wasteful and meaningless.

Tim worked as an engineer, and Jean was a psych aide in a ward for abused children.

They both went to bed early in order to get their eight hours of sleep each night. Intercourse once every other week was all right. Clothed intercourse with the lights off, lasting only minutes, in the standard position. Both were partial to quick kisses. Neither liked the tongue.

Jean shivered. "Well, why didn't you call me? Why didn't you check on me? All those kids I work with. I had to keep them sane."

"You know I don't have your work number."

"You never asked for it, Tim."

"I never needed it. You have your mom if something really happened."

"And your brother lives right down the street."

"And he called me."

"To ask if I called you?"

"No, Jean, he called to see if I was all right, like you were supposed to do."

Tim came from a good-sized Irish Catholic family. His mother was just two miles away in thehouse he grew up in. Two married sisters in Delaware.

"If I was living with you, I would have called you," she said.

"Why would you move in here with me? This is an hour from your work."

"We could live together some place."

"I'm not selling my house. Not in this market. And what about your mother? You can't leave her alone after all these years...so where are we going, huh?" He sounded irritated. The icy range in his voice. "Jean, what if I said I will marry you tomorrow?"

A white chill bit through her. She folded her lips.

"You wouldn't ask me that."

"What if I did? What if I said, 'Jean, let's get married'. What would you do then?"

He turned to her. "Look, maybe I'll get that new position. I'll be able to telecommute. I'll also make about $10,000 more."

"Then we'd see more of each other?"

He lapsed into thoughtful silence.

They lay silent as if watching a dying fire. No chasing after each other crying. The arguments they had were never operatic. They were always like this, carefully modulated.

She pulled the covers more tightly over her nightgowned body. He seemed fine in his flannel pjs. Some people are like that, climatized.

The next morning, Jean drove home, looking without watching, without seeing. She thought of all those glossy vacation brochures she'd been collecting, fantasizing about their imaginary honeymoon where they would both finally splurge and live it up. She'd also been scoping out children with olive complexions and straight hair. That's how her pretend child looked. Straight-haired. No turn at all. She wasn't a racist; she just liked that look. She believed it was prettier.

Jean never thought she was particularly pretty. Her thick eyebrows dipped into a V. All through high school, her mother wouldn't let her pluck her eyebrows. If her mother would've let her pluck her eyebrows, would she have been more popular back then? Those were the crucial years for forming relations. All of the expectant widows of 9/11 seemed so well connected. Well into family formation when it happened. Several were in their ninth month of pregnancy.

She stopped for gasoline and a Snowball. Jean liked to write down everything she spent through the day, right down to the sixty-six-cent cupcake purchase. In her whole life, she'd never bought a bottle of wine or dry-cleaned an outfit. She had cassettes. No CDs. That would mean buying a CD player. Her clothes were from Clover's. Sensible shoes, not too much heel. She really hadn't changed her simple style of dress from 20 years ago.

The sugar and carbohydrates plateau took away her headache. Up until that day, Jean had thought that he was the one. They had so much in common. Both were conservative people. Though it was mid-November and they'd been going out over a year, Tim wasn't her boyfriend. They didn't share. She never left anything over his house, or felt like she could – should.

When Jean reached Calhoun, the small, nondescript borough on the outskirts of Philadelphia, her mother was about to leave for Presbyterian Church. Her blue haired, gossipy friends were about to come by for her. The house was roasting. Her mother liked to keep things at 77, fussing at her anytime she touched the thermostat. Jean immediately took off layers of clothing till she was just in an undershirt.

Jean stirred some Tang into a glass of water and put the Eggos in the toaster.

"Why don't you have some oatmeal today, Jean?"

"I don't want oatmeal."

"You have waffles every morning. Have pancakes. It's almost the same."

"I want waffles, Mom."

Jean's mom had shiny black walnut skin and a Jeri curl wig that she started to wear after a bad relaxer. "What movie did you see? Did you see Collateral Damage? Is it worth it or is it a rental?" she asked her daughter.

"It was all right, Ma," Jean answered.

"I thought they were holding that back because of all this."

"They did. It was originally supposed to be released back in September."

"Well, I guess enough time has passed. Here it is November already. Does he get the terrorist that killed his family?"

"Of course, Ma. That's Hollywood."

"I wish you would have waited to see it with me, Jean. I like Schwartzenagger."

"We can see the next thing he's in, Mom."

Jean was an only child; the product of her father's second marriage. She had half brothers and sisters that were in their fifties and a whole cadre of half nieces and nephews who lived from 200 to 1000 miles away. It was hard to keep in touch. Her happiest days were behind her—when she was really young, watching her father adjusting the Windsor knot of his tie. Wrapped in a quilt of her father memories, missing his large, big knuckled hands – his laughter. He liked coconut-covered, marshmallow-filled cupcakes. It was adult-onset diabetes he'd died of. He kept his sickness from her.

He was that kind of father.

Jean reassured herself that Tim wouldn't break up with her with the holidays coming. He was sensible enough save the trouble of looking for someone new. So, another whole generic year went by, almost, and Jean and Tim were on the same tepid schedule. Once a week dinner or movie/ sex barely touching. But it didn't feel like the relationship was winding down. It was just settling down, like a stone at the bottom of a river. Eggos and Tang. Day after day, Jean went to work, came home and spoke to her mother and went to bed.

International news varied in the next few months. It was either about anti-terrorist military squads or the INS or whatever. Yet it never seemed like the culprits would be precisely identified. Months later, the bad guys weren't captured. They hid in caves. Jean didn't read the New York Times. She watched TV and Peter Jennings told her and her mom about Afghanistan and other countries she'd never heard of. What was Al Quada? What's a Jihad? This vocabulary. This geography.

Ten months passed, everyone was still asking deep questions about kismet. What's kismet? Jean wanted to find a new job, but was unable to locate the resolve to do so. She didn't even want to be in the educational field anymore. She never did. Obedient and logical, she had done beautifully in high school, but less so in college, where her brand of spewing back exactly what was dictated to her wasn't so well-rewarded. Her papers would always come back with the same advice: "Put more you into this."

She should have gone to forestry school. That's what she really wanted to do, but there were so few women in the field and even fewer blacks. As a consolation, she volunteered at an animal shelter Saturday mornings and afternoons. She liked feeding cats and dogs. She liked helping the approved applicants select just the right dog for adoption. She had her eye on a Labrador retriever mix. Just two months. Dogs stay in your life for a decade or so. It'd be like a marriage. She ran the idea past her mom.

"I don't want some dog," her mom said.

"It's a small dog, Mom."

"Who's going to clean up after it? You? Look how you keep your room."

Jean listened to her mom as she'd always done. Her mom was now in her 70s. A little stooped, she took tablets for her osteoporosis. It was her house. Jean just lived there with her. Her mother set the thermostat high, saying old people have old bones.

The first September 11th was on a Tuesday. This time it fell on a Wednesday. Jean called Tim.

"Hi," she said.

"Hello," he said.

"I just wanted to call you."

"What? Why?"

"Because I didn't last year."

"Oh, that. You're still thinking about that. That's ancient history. I'm glad you called...I have to go away this weekend. So we can't get together."

She thought of how it would be like lying in bed with him. Not touching, not looking at each other in their frozen divorced compartments.

"Isn't it funny? Your bother got married to that girl who he'd known for six months less than you'd known me."

"That's funny?"

Jean was burning up in this hot house. "I didn't get to the punchline—they still haven't found Bin Laden."

41

"You're acting strange."

"Aren't you going to ask how work was today?"

"You never asked me. Look, where is all this going, Jean? You call me in the middle of this week, and you're all over the place."

"Have a good trip, Tim. I'll see you the weekend you get back."

"Now you sound like yourself, Jean. Good night."

Then he hung up. Then she hung up.

It was only eight in the evening. She looked around the room to see horse posters on the wall.

They'd been there since 6th grade. Jean walked downstairs.

Her mom was on the couch. Sunday paper still out. Metro section strewn. A 9/11 retrospective of local residents lost. Coupons clipped.

Her mother had coffee on a saucer. No longer hot, lukewarm. Cold. Jean wondered how she could stand sipping at it. Cold liquid that was supposed to be hot.

Her mom had her hands on the remote scanning the channels. Press the bottom on the control, and the image faded.

On this anniversary, Jean didn't want to be alone. She went to the kitchen to have Ritz crackers with peanut butter, and then she went to the living room to be with her mother. A sofa and two armchairs formed a U around the TV.

"I guess nothing regular's going to come on tonight," her mother muttered.

A young, hot Latin singer did his hit single. Something about being a hero. It was clear that his vocal ability was lacking. He made it on his appearance. Tall, olive, romantic looking.

"What kind of variety show is this?" her mother asked.

Jean sighed, leaned in the doorway, and turned her eyes toward the set. In that chunk of time after her father passed away and she had started going out with Tim, she questioned life. Obviously, those who die young never grow old, but how about those who grow old who never had the chance to be young? Jean was young when her father passed.

Jean wanted a new life. She wanted death to the one that she had. With any death, there would be rejection of the truth, depression from the truth, acceptance, then the reconstruction part. She needed to change towns and jobs. She needed to buy a place to live on her own. But she didn't want to live alone. She couldn't.

When her father died, the world didn't stop. TV shows weren't preempted. Balding, overweight, always had a smile, joked a lot. He used to bring home Chinese food and Chinese tea and say "Take tea, and see." Upon his death, her legs buckled under, face frozen in disbelief. His laugh, big, throaty and full. He was the life of the house. He lived 72 years, six months, and twenty-two days.

Jean's heavily-lidded eyes watched the TV. She thought that she could try to find someone else on the internet. Log on under her America On Line handle. Her middle name followed by the number 2. Perhaps she could meet someone who actually wanted to share. To get married and have a child and a dog. To start something that would be there. Always.

It was the pop opera singer's turn. The way this woman sang was so emotive and clear. She reached her arms and delivered a song from the musical Carousel. "You'll…never… walk… alone…" The camera panned the audience of blacks, whites, youngs, olds, gentiles, Jews.

The audience nodded in affirmation. They turned to their sons and daughters and sisters and brothers like this was just what they needed to hear.

Jean's right ear touched the flat cushion. Her shoulders sagged. She felt life pass her, and then she felt nothing.

Craig Evenson is a school teacher. His poems have appeared in such magazines as *Midwest Quarterly*, *Paper Nautilus*, and *Cafe Review*. He has work forthcoming in *West Trade Review* and *Lost Coast Review*. He lives in Minnesota.

Natural Causes

In dusty houses
with sallow shades
floating ghostly
past books, pictures,
broken furniture

unconnected
disengaged

Functional rubble
of teeth, knees, hips,
skipping the charters to Branson,
afternoon performances
of Romeo and Juliet

writing in their journals
how the view from the end of the road
mirrors the view from the beginning:
a thoughtless line
vining to mind,
a heart of treetops,
vanishing unsurprised
through the floorboards.

Christos Kallis born in Larnaca, Cyprus, is currently studying for his undergraduate degree in English Literature at the University of Glasgow. He is active in the English and American poetry scene, and he is always trying to broaden his network. Recently his poems have appeared or are forthcoming in *the London Journal of Fiction*, *Stoneboat*, *The Hartskill Review*, *TulipTree Review*, *Prole*, among others.

Between Monologues

When the eyes are no longer open
To interpretation, hold the moment
In your palm before the moment
Cascades. Words that you've been
Missing from the scene, will come
Late, but the problem seems to be
That you haven't experienced flirting
Until, like my mother says, you've
Flirted with a caesura. It's funny the
Way your bodies look like banana
Peels and funny that she slipped
On you and you slept on her. Quite
Tragic, I thought, that all your life
You've been tracking lips on thighs,
And how shocking it was when you
Found out that lips have always been
On the face. You are still embarrassed,
And you shouldn't be, that she caught
You apologizing to your body parts
Three years ago. You still remember
That day as if it was right now. You
Can remember that the room was no
Longer lighted by the lava lamp,
And before she caught you, the lava
Escaped the lamp, and then you had
To face open eyes that interpret you.

Enjoyed this issue of *Sunset Liminal*? Be on the lookout for Volume IV, coming out Fall 2016!

If you want to have a shot at having your work featured in the next issue of *Sunset Liminal*, e-mail up to 5000 words of prose or up to five poems as .doc or .docx attachments to **sunsetliminal@gmail.com** with either "Prose Submissions" or "Poetry Submissions" in the subject line.

If you're interested in learning more, like us on Facebook and follow us on Tumblr and Twitter.

http://www.facebook.com/sunsetliminalpress/
http://www.sunsetliminal.tumblr.com/
http://twitter.com/SunsetLiminal/

www.ingramcontent.com/pod-product-compliance
Lightning Source LLC
Chambersburg PA
CBHW050951030426
42339CB00007B/378